Just My Thoughts...

ISBN 978-1-67810-949-

90000

9 781678 109493

Patience

It's hard, I know.

Seeing everyone else prospering in love, in life, in career paths...

It's hard I know.

Working so hard and not getting results or recognition.

Doing everything it takes to prove your worth, your skill set, yourself.

It's hard I know.

Keeping positive and keeping your head above water all on your own. Finding the joy in the little things can feel impossible.

It gets better though.

Rome wasn't built in a day... it took 1,009,491 days and it was an empire forever remembered in history. One of my favorite and strongest trees is the sequoia tree. This giant, magnificent tree takes 20 years to reach its full potential and can continue to grow even after.

It takes time though.

Nothing worth having or doing comes easy or will be easy. Failure makes us human. Persevering makes us stronger. Perfection is unattainable. Success hits us when we're least expecting it just like all good things do.

It takes patience.

It's hard, I know.

Nothing is worse than feeling like the worlds against you and your time is well past due.

 It gets better though.

Good things come to those who wait. Cherish everything you have because there's always someone worse off than you.

It takes time though. It's worth it, I promise it is. Keep doing whatever it is you do.

It takes patience.

Take a deep breath ... in ... out... go.

Worth It

It's like a vice around my neck constantly tightening by the second.

The lack of oxygen blurs my vision and causes my insides to collapse...

It breaks my soul and kills every nerve till I'm numb to the core....

It brings me to my breaking point.

Some days I feel like I'm just here.

Like I'm just existing and not actually living... there are days I just want to stay in bed or crawl in a hole and let myself be forgotten

But a kiss from you breaks that vice.

It clears my vision & sparks life all through my body... it lifts my soul & ignites this fire inside me. It makes my knees weak but the rest of me feel so strong & shows me life is worth sticking around for.

You make me feel alive, you make me feel like I matter, and you make me feel important. Your kind words and beautiful smile makes getting up easier...

Makes it worth it.

Naked

You undress me with your words

Touch me with your eyes

You make me cum with your voiced opinions

& my ultimate climax comes when you listen.

Your corny jokes impress me & you let me be moody.

You let me laugh as loud as I please & you keep my head above water.

You wipe my tears before they even fall & you allow me to be me.

The best part is you do all this while my clothes are still on.

You don't need to take them off.

You just listen... & respond... & care... then suddenly I'm naked with you.

Alone

Alone... all alone.

It's not even a feeling anymore, it's a state of being. I don't feel alone I just know I am.

I know by the stares, the longing to be a part of something, the desire to have the relationships I see others share.

But those things aren't meant for me.

Because I'm alone... & that's what I'm best at being.

Alone... all alone.

No one bothers to take my feelings into account, let alone my thoughts.

What I say or feel is irrelevant, no one is truly here to help they just like to pretend they are.

Alone ... that's me.

In a room full of people blind to my pain. Silently screaming to be noticed or to even be thought of.

But those things aren't meant for me.

I'm forgotten.

I'm mistreated.

I'm out casted.

It all makes sense though, I don't belong.

That's that.

I'm better off alone... all alone.

Insecurities

You're bad for me, I know it.

Yet every morning I find myself waking you up to start the day with me.

Making sure you're well fed as I critique myself inch by inch until I'm disgusted with myself.

Then I give you the full report so you can make notes and plan on when you're going to bring them up.

You're bad for me I know it.

Yet every afternoon I invite you & you never fail to show face.

You make sure I notice the girl wearing her short shorts carelessly, how clean & unscarred her skin remains.

You make sure I pay attention to all the things I wish I could be.

You're bad for me, I know it.

Yet every night you make your presence known in my dreams... or once again in my mirror standing beside me.

Pointing... observing... criticizing...

Belittling me as I put my hair up to wash my face.

Another day of not being enough.

Another day of finding something to hate about myself.

Another day of allowing my demons to win.

No matter what you heard, impossible is just a word.

I wish I could see it.

Everyone talks about it.

Everyone claims to see it.

Why can't I?

I chose not to, that's why.

I don't allow myself that gratification because it's always been a façade.

"You're beautiful but..."

But...

I wish I knew why I'm never enough...

Why everyone says I deserve the world yet no one wants to give it to me.

I choose to isolate myself ... that's why

I don't want anyone telling people they gave me something I couldn't give myself...

"I love you but"

But...

I couldn't fathom why those words were spoken if they weren't genuine.

Fairies Exist

Fairies exist.

There's no magical forest or make believe world.

This world itself is full of life & beautiful creatures. I was told to live life because that's what we were put here to do.

To love, to share, to prosper.

Fairies exist because it's not logically plausible to say we know what's out there when we've yet to discover ourselves entirely.

Her Voice

As I set out on another trip for bricks to strengthen my wall I was stopped by a voice.

She said she'd help me collect bricks as long as I told her why I needed them.

I agreed then began to tell her a story of love, devotion, betrayal, and lessons.

She listened quietly, understood my tale of sorrows & woes & simply made me laugh.

Her confident voice calmed my crashing waves.

Her bright smile led me out of the dark.

Her presence eased my souls longing for love.

I looked down to find I hadn't picked up a single brick, but she had.

As I spoke she let me feel…

She let me stutter…

She let my wounds bleed and she waited for my voice to stop trembling…

Then she built me up.

She took the bricks and built me a throne instead of a wall.

A throne to be cherished, to sit on and be admired on… a throne so I knew I was something worth learning. Something worth believing in. I found myself listening to her voice & finding peace.

Now I set out on trips but now I search for flowers for my crown because I should be something to love not lock away… something to look at, not pass by.

Her voice stays… it stays and I love it.

The Flower

Unselfish.

A gardener must be selfless.

His flowers need his love and his patience to grow.

Unselfish.

A woman needs someone that's selfless.

Her heart needs love and patience to grow.

Like a flower you must water her, nurture her, and protect her.

She is delicate and one of a kind and must be treated as such.

Unselfish.

That's the only way you'll obtain her love...

That's the only way you'll help her grow.

If you could hold me where would your hands wander?

Where would your mind stray?

I want a love with no doubts.

No need for safety nets or empty apologies, I want security.

To know I'm theirs & all they desire.

The longing I feel for the love I crave frustrates me.

I hate the thought of needing someone but as humans it's normal.

Normal to crave stability, normal to dream of that story book love, normal to face disappointment.

But the new norm has become a game of heartless actions, a competition to see who can execute their mischievous intentions without being caught first.

There's no loyalty or respect... no regards for the consequences of their actions.

To be yourself with someone else is beauty in its purest form.

People are told to conform and fall in line.

Those that dance to their own beat and flow freely through life are the bravest among us.

In a world that shuns others for viewing things differently it's refreshing.

Refreshing like her lips after a long day

Intoxicating like her touch is straight patron.

Dreams weren't something she took lightly; they were real to her.

Even if she didn't fulfil them right that moment, she kept her faith and found reality was her dream as long as she made it so.

She is me.

People told me to conform and fall in line.

But I make my own beats and like the win I go where I please without fear.

Full of a world that only knows judgment and ridicule, my impact is pure.

To be myself with someone else is the only way I know, love my entirety or let me be.

As milk and honey flow through your lips I feel your hands grip my thighs and wander to my chest...

My back arches... my body rises with each stroke of your tongue and my moans are cut short by your hand constricting my throat.

This is bliss

This is real

This is pleasure

Your lips release me and you hover over me, staring me dead in my eyes as your other had finds its way between my lips... she swallows one... Two... three of your fingers and embraces them repeatedly as if begging for more.

As your fingers curl, my eyes roll and my body quivers under your touch.

My scars tell my story.

I don't always want them to but even when I'm caught off guard I've learned to be open with my past.

You never know what the next person might be going through.

Maybe they have scars too and need to be reminded that they're not alone.

Maybe they don't have any scars but they've had thoughts and need a voice to tell them there's better ways.

As I looked in the mirror, I could see the changes...

The healed scars, the fresh healing scars, but I knew.

I knew they each held their own story and that they told my life through my body, I am art.

I smiled knowing that these scars are with my soul and anyone that can see and love me for them is just as beautiful as me.

Delicate

Delicate… her heart. Her mind, her words.

They're a rare find & if you're lucky enough to encounter her be careful.

She's delicate.

I was blindsided... completely unaware of what was happening.

I didn't know you were someone I'd want in my life even on the worst days.

I never knew I'd miss you saying my name because it's my name, I've heard it my whole life but no one ever made it sound so euphoric.

I never thought I'd miss your laugh after I went 20 years without hearing it... how could it haunt me in my loneliest moments?

I was blindsided... completely unaware of what was happening.

I never knew you would be someone I'd reminisce about even on the worst days.

I didn't know you wore a mask because it fit you so well, I was convinced you were just that perfect naturally.

I didn't think you could lie so sweetly because your words flowed with such ease... how could they touch me so gently yet cut me so deeply?

I wasn't blindsided... I was completely aware of what was happening.

I knew your love was conditional and fragile even on our best days.

I knew you weren't as obsessed with me as you wanted me to believe, I'd noticed that I only had your attention when the sun set and you were lonely.

I knew I wasn't the woman of your dreams especially when you tossed & turned while you laid beside me... how could you not want my love when that's all I wanted to give you?

I wasn't blindsided ... I was completely aware of what was happening.

I was merely a pawn for you to play with till you reached your queen, I was never a part of the bigger scheme.

I was there for your comfort when she couldn't be, it was obvious but you were a great fabricator and I was wrapped up in your lies because they kept me so warm while I journeyed through the most algor darkness my being has experienced.

I knew better ... but no one ever made the path to heartbreak seem so inviting.

Fresh

Times are changing and so is the journey. A new door is unlocked & as it opens I'm blasted with warmth.

Flowers are blooming as far as the eye can see... its green & full & the waters are rushing, surging through the hills of green... it brings life to everything around it.

Traced by God's own finger the stream flows down a winding path & as I climb into my boat & grab my paddles, I pause.

I breathe in my surroundings & let my vessel flow with the current.

He knows what he has in store for me & all he asked me to do was trust.

I lay down my paddles... at last... my journey begins.

Blue Butterfly

Smiles and laughter surround me.

Their love wraps me up like a mother does her new born baby... I'm held tight for countless nights.

Every moment feels like a push of reassurance that things will work out.

I felt frail and fresh ... filled with a new sense of purpose and meaning but still leaning on my pillars of strength.

My yellow butterfly whose wings carry me through chaotic storms.

My red cardinal whose bold red feathers remind me of my strength in times of conflict.

My blue jay that keeps me smiling when I'm in search of fulfillment of understanding.

They help guide me out of my cocoon & protect me until my wings have dried.

Wings as blue as the sky, I blend as I take flight.

Listen

I have broken my silence.

I have seen the impact my thoughts have when someone takes the time to understand them.

Silence, though sometimes necessary, is not something I want to be remembered for.

I believe in the power I've been given to heal and love others... I used to fight it but this is who I was made to be.

If you can keep up with my mental, I can open my mind and share my stories.

I can share what I've learned and what new perspectives I've tried.

I can share what failed and what worked and even if they choose to follow their own advice, I know my guidance was offered.

I shed my light on even the smallest moments hoping to make any kind of impact.

I will not stand by.

I refuse to let others think they're going through these trials alone.

Let my scars speak their truths to your soul.

Coexisting

A rare find.

Someone that could keep up with my thoughts, my ramblings, my overly passionate outbursts at things most see as insignificant.

Then there she was... She dissected my brain to the point that I needed a moment to process the way my eyes had just been opened to a concept the rest of my conscious found delight in meditating on.

My ramblings were met by an active ear.

She listened to each point being made even when they weren't entirely lucid.

What left me speechless more than anything was the aptness of the way she was able to decipher even my most unusual propositions.

She watched as I let my seemingly effortless work turn into a labyrinthine of unsubstantial distress, I could do nothing but wander through.

Then she would go out and cut through my labyrinthine with empathy and admiration, never judgement or skepticism.

Her heart was indeed a rare find for a rare belle.

A Bee Sting

When faced with despondency often times we allow it to fester in us. When that happens that seed of pessimism is fueled by every distressing occurrence that follows, until finally we find ourselves erupting under the disturbance of a feather.

However, if you look at the misadventure in the same light you do a bee sting you'd see that it has no power over you unless you allow it.

Of course it hurts, burns even at first... but once you sit down and remove the stinger you automatically start to feel better.

As time passes you think less and less about the initial sting.

Next thing you know you're telling someone about your day and you laugh when you recap your bee story.

When we deal with our struggles head on, we kill that seed from ever sprouting.

Remove the stinger, take some time to think on it, then share your story.

Fight the oppression with light and love.

A Heart of Gold

When I'm told by others that I possess a heart of gold they think it's a compliment.

And maybe to them it is, but if only they knew the weight of this seemingly grand asset...

If only they knew how many times a heart has to be broken before it turns to gold...

There's times that it feels as if my chest were on fire and in danger of caving in...

But still I had love to give to others around me and when I filled them with my love sometimes they filled me with theirs in return ... most times they wouldn't.

There's just one rule… honesty.

You never lie to me; I know exactly what you're thinking because you tell me willingly.

You're opinionated… you're strong… you're your own person.

Your presence alone demands others attention, demands my attention.

I'm willingly submissive to you and it's all out of respect.

"No" isn't a word we use often because support is far from sparse when it comes to me and you.

Beautiful isn't it?

The mind.

Where anything may happen and everything can be.

It's our greatest asset and is often neglected.

You must stimulate your brain.

Allow it to rest and take in the true beauties of life.

A literal stop and smell the roses.

I want to be kissed in the rain, movie style.

A hopeless romantic indeed.

My Waves

I'm one with the water.

I feel free yet contained.

I know parts of me will touch people without trying to and I know I can be both a blessing and a curse.

The same way I help others I destroy myself.

I give because I have but once I start to run dry any thoughts of rationing are non-existent. Coincidentally no one else thinks to stop taking.

I am strong but sensitive. A small pebble can make ripples that stick with me for longer than they should but my current sweeps people away with such ease it's almost amusing.

Yet because you see my shake at a pebble, you forget my soundness.

A crash of my waves on the shore is my subtle reminder to you.

Trust

It's scary, I know. Trusting another person with your heart.

Allowing yourself to be vulnerable will never be an easy thing to do but sometimes we trust just enough to let them see us as we truly are.

Flaws and all, a naked soul, and the faith we have in the idea of love.

All crystal clear for that someone that knows it's them you believe in to hold you so delicately.

Trust is such a fragile yet strong thing.

When you trust someone completely it's beautiful... it's what I imagine lyrics to a song feel like.

A perfect fit, made for one another.

And when it's pure it's not easily broken because together, they know how to protect it because of their devotion to one another... it's scary, yes... but oh so beautiful.

Say It

To believe in something means to put your faith into it and do whatever it takes to see it unfold.

Speaking it into existence is key.

Say it. Whatever it is you want for yourself & your life, say it.

You must be your number one fan because sometimes you have to be.

It won't be easy and the journey is a long one but you were made to reach limits you never dreamed of & I know this because each of us has purpose.

We're set on a path with detours and rest stops but as long as we trust and love ourselves throughout any struggles or trials we face we will make it to our destination.

Even if no one ever believed you could, you did... and that's all it took.

Her name tastes like a rich dessert as it passes through my lips.

Each movement my mouth takes to utter her name is like each note to a melody and it causes my soul to dance.

Her name is my safe word.

My sanctuary.

Her name brings my wildest fires to mere embers that glow like fireflies darting in the darkest skies.

The same way it soothes me it excites me.

Pure ecstasy fills my mind and my valley pours the purest water for her.

The thought of singing her name in praise while holding her head in place causes my heart to lose its rhythm.

It causes my body to fill with the warmth of a thousand sun's...

Her name gives me hope... Her name is my desire.

Seatbelt

Held close by my grasp, you feel safe with me.

You trust me unquestionably, you're yourself with me.

I've held you through tears that fell during moments of sorrow and slow songs that set the mood for the rainy drive ahead.

I've held you through drunken nights and listened to every word of your intoxicated ramblings discovering each time that your mind is its own galaxy.

I've held you during laughing fits with your friends and the hot coffee that ruined your shirt in traffic on the way to work.

Yet even though I hold you during your most dire times you still only use me in your time of need.

A Camel

The distance is no problem for me.

I've always loved the scenic route.

See I was built for endurance, to travel to the regions others tremble at the thought of exploring.

I'd journey to the ends of the world for your pleasure if you willed me to.

Like a camel I am constructed to withstand the most discordant of environments...

The stars as my guide my body and soul finds peace when I follow the maps of the sky.

I only wish to aid you along this treacherous journey we call life.

I long for the honor of being your protector and your beacon to a place of felicity.

Won't you let me guide you? The distance is no issue for me.

Gem

When you think of me you know my beauty, but you know nothing of my struggles.

You think I became who I am overnight?

I went through the fire and I lasted through the pressure.

I didn't fold when I was chosen and I don't see failure in my future.

I was molded by time, patience, determination.

I am an instrument of success and an ambassador for genuine life.

I was once nothing more than a rock of the Earth but now I am a gem.

I'm torn, how do I know when it's the right person?

They say you just know... but how?

We meet countless people throughout our lifetimes and it seems as if all of them promise things they know they won't deliver...

Everything seems temporary.

How do I know..?

After so many have shown me they aren't what they said they were why would I become okay with loving them?

Settling for something that might be good for me doesn't appeal to my nature.

I don't want to fall just to bust my ass again...

But what if they catch me this time?

You come around when you want, not when I need you.

You always take more than you give.

I bet you can't even spell equal.

I've been through this before and I can tell you the script like a read through.

See because you're selfish, you're self-absorbed...

You only care when it's your voice that's being heard.

Doubting

When others doubt you, it hurts.

When you doubt yourself its self-inflicted agony.

Wondering why you aren't enough.

Good enough.

Strong enough.

Pure enough.

When others doubt you it's as if their words are stingers that can be removed.

When you doubt yourself it's like a dagger in your heart that can't be removed without fatal consequences.

Open Up

I've seen the cage you built for yourself...

Did you think that would stop the pain?

Pain lives in us and feeds solidarity.

That's how it festers within us, it sits and lets you water it with your self-doubt, lack of self-love, and pattern of shutting down when things get a little chaotic.

That's how you get trapped in that cage...

Like flowers, weeds grow... and when their leaves grow, they form vines.

These vines have laced themselves throughout every hole and bar in order to keep that cage inescapable.

Now you're left to think of nothing more than your sorrows and fuck ups as you sit in this too small cage that only gets smaller the more you tend to it...

I've seen the cage you built for yourself...

Did you think that would stop the pain?

Pain lives there with you, you've made it a home.

Just String

Like a cat with a ball of string you toy with me.

You run your hands over my body, dragging your claws down my back.

You push me left and bump me right, rolling me on my side... on my back.

You make me think you want me by stripping me down eagerly with your tongue.

You put emphasis on every action... every word.

I'm under your control as you slowly peel away at every layer I'm composed of.

You wait till I'm helpless under your touch and begging for more of this maliciously intriguing game of yours.

Then... you stop.

You get tired of your actions and you forget your desires for me.

Then... there I am.

Half undone, completely unsatisfied... but still craving the next moment I might feel your touch.

Like a moth to a flame, I let myself be tempted...

I gaze into your light... your eyes... and I lose my train of thought.

The same way a flame engulfs its victims you wrap around me till I'm covered and can do nothing but crumble under your power.

You offer me sweet release but take it away as soon as I get within reach.

Like a cat with a ball of string you toy with me.

Then once I'm undone, you forget me again, I'm no longer your concern because now I'm just string.

Uncertainty

There's moments I can't help but think about life... I rack my brain for answers, create realistic and unrealistic scenarios, I drown myself in doubt.

I can't help myself some days... I try to switch my thoughts but they always find their way back to the same topic... what's next?

I can't stop life from happening of course... I just wish I could see a glimpse of why or maybe what...

I'd never change my past because then the lessons I've learned would be lost along with my erased memories.

In these moments though I feel as though my heads underwater... filling up with too much for me to handle... it burns, I scream... it's pointless.

It can never be heard over the waves crashing inside my brain.

I'm muted but only externally.

Internally me, myself, and I battle the monsters that continue to tear away at my precious brain.

My Demons

I don't know how to share my demons...

They're too viscous sometimes and I fear I may pass them on to someone else unintentionally...

I don't know how to keep them caged either...

It's not their faut they're so malicious, life has treated them just as it does everyone.

They're taken for a joke.

Said to be "caused by the longing for attention"... and yet they all came to me to ask for mine so how could I refuse... no one ever listened to me and I refused to be deaf to bleeding hearts so I listened... only I got in too deep.

Now they take turns trying to take charge when they're feeling their egos.

I told them they could stay till we figured out a solution to their misery... I didn't realize they'd make such sturdy homes.

I was certain I could help them but I forgot I couldn't even help myself yet...

That would take me some time to realize though and by then they'd taken over.

Multiplied like rabbits and grew like beanstalks, tall and green with envy of my physical being...

They were stronger together than I was alone and they knew it... so they kept it that way.

Her

Her eyes are like mahogany... they're strong & emulate the purest chocolate ever made.

When her eyes meet mine, I can feel her rooting herself in the deepest parts of my soul & it feels enlightening... her roots drink me in.

Her arms are like vines... they're sturdy & they entangle me in the most comforting way.

When her arms embrace me, I can feel her guarding me from my demons & their loathsome scrutiny... her vines hold me in a state of nirvana.

Her smile is like a clam with its pearl... its radiance brings light to even the smallest of moments.

When she flashed her jewel, my heart was enticed to the point that I've found myself absorbed in it.

Everything about her is bewitching & secure ... she makes loving feel effortless yet she puts forth so much effort.

When she's in my presence my words escape me & all I can grasp is the certainty that she's a dream come true & I never want to wake from it.

Clean Hands

Wash your hands before you handle me,
Carefully you must caress me.
Impurities attempt to feed on my flesh,
This is why you must heed my request.

My being is delicate.
My mind awaits, celibate.
Waiting to be unlocked by the right exposition.
To gain access to my extensive ideations.

Wash your hands before you handle me.
Because I've been handled carelessly.
Their impurities fed vigorously on my flesh
And I was screaming at them to notice the mess.

My being is sacred.
My heart longs for safeness.
Waiting to be appreciated by the right infatuation,
To experience a love without limitation.

Wash your hands before you handle me.

The Victim

I've been the victim for so long I forgot my power.

I made myself the victim in situations where I HAD the power... just because I didn't believe I did.

At times I procrastinate, I talk a great game and very seldom back it up when it comes to my dreams.
I'm confused and uncertain and that scares me to the core.

I don't know who I am... not entirely.
But I do know I am NOT a victim.

ISBN 978-1-67810-949-

9 781678 109493

90000

www.ingramcontent.com/pod-product-compliance
Lightning Source LLC
Chambersburg PA
CBHW022347040426
42449CB00006B/753